Loading the Ship

Written by Lisa Thompson

Pictures by Craig Smith

Here comes a barrel of water.

The Captain takes
one gold coin
out of his pocket.

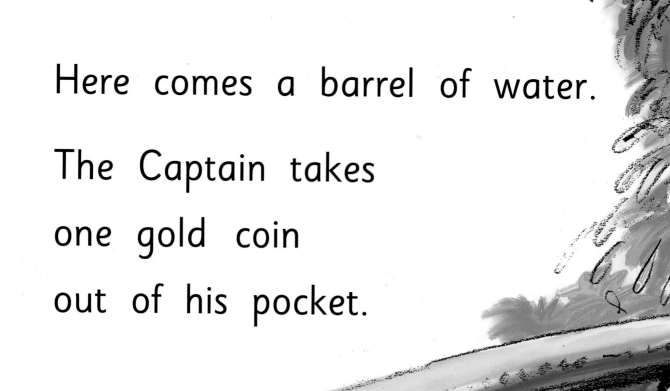

Here comes a barrel of flour.

The Captain takes
two gold coins
out of his pocket.

Here comes a barrel of rice.

The Captain takes
three gold coins
out of his pocket.

Here comes a barrel of biscuits.

The Captain takes
four gold coins
out of his pocket.

Here comes a barrel of sweets.

The Captain takes
five gold coins
out of his pocket.

Here comes a barrel
of ice-cream.

The Captain takes
six gold coins
out of his pocket.

13

Here comes a barrel of mice!

The captain keeps his
hands in his pockets.